York has one of the finest China shops

Mulberry Hall

Mulberry Hall takes particular pride in two things: its premises, one of the best medieval buildings in the ancient city of York; and its reputation, as one of the best shops in Europe for fine china and crystal.

Mulberry Hall's 12 showrooms extend over three floors. They are given over to an unsurpassed display of the best which England and Europe have to offer, supported by stock in depth.

Porcelain: Wedgwood, Spode, Royal Doulton, Royal Worcester, Royal Crown Derby, Coalport, Royal Copenhagen, Herend, Aynsley.
Crystal: Stuart, Waterford, Baccarat, Lalique, Edinburgh.
Enamels: Halcyon Days.

Mulberry Hall
Fine china & crystal specialists
Stonegate York YO1 2AW England
Telephone 0904 20736

A page of Britain's favourite

British Sugar is the UK's top producer of sugar, a pure and natural high-energy food. Every year we process sugar beet to provide more than a million tonnes of Silver Spoon Sugar, as well as over half a million tonnes of animal feeds.

British Sugar is a significant force in the community. The company employs around 6,000 people in the UK, and supports thousands more jobs in allied industries such as agriculture, transport and engineering.

Silver Spoon accounts for more than half the sugar consumed each year in the UK. Simply bags of energy.

BRITISH SUGAR plc
PO Box 26, Oundle Road, Peterborough PE2 9QU

YORK

THE OFFICIAL GUIDE

THE
HISTORY
OF
YORK
IS THE
HISTORY
OF
ENGLAND.

King George VI

¶

Published by the City of York

Copyright – York City Council. Published 1987 ISBN 0 903 281 02 3

· THE OFFICIAL GUIDE · TO YORK

Lantern Tower,
York Minster
¶

· INTRODUCTION ·

During its 1900 turbulent years of history, York has been at the centre of many world shaping events. It was built by the Romans at the height of their empire, conquered by the Anglo-Saxons and ruled by the Vikings. The city was ravaged by William the Conqueror, nearly crushed by Henry VIII and besieged by Cromwell. Despite all this, York was for centuries a great religious centre and the northern capital of England.

A city that gave birth to both the revered Emperor Constantine the Great and St. Margaret of York, as well as to the notorious Guy Fawkes and Dick Turpin.

Today, York is one of the best preserved medieval cities in Europe, as vibrant and alive as it was 1900 years ago. Come, explore, discover and revel in the delights of the magical, historical, timeless City of York.

3½ million bars sold every day in the U.K.

All made in York

· EBORACUM ·
ROMAN YORK

In the years before the Roman invasion of Britain in A.D. 43, the entire area from the Humber River to the Firth of Forth was ruled by a powerful confederation of Celtic tribes known as the Brigantes. Recent archaeological evidence suggests that these Iron Age people had a settlement at York, which the ancient historian Ptolemy called "Eborakon."

In A.D. 71 the Roman Governor of Britain, Quintus Petillius Cerialis, led his troops northward from Lincoln to invade "Brigantia." Recognizing a good military strongpoint, he based his camp at the juncture of two rivers, the Ouse and the Foss. The Brigantes were subdued and the Roman Ninth Legion built a permanent fortress on the site of their temporary camp, calling it "Eboracum."

Eventually the fortress walls enclosed fifty acres and housed a garrison of six thousand soldiers. New roads were laid down to link up with existing ones. A civilian town grew up outside the fortress and "Eboracum" became one of the leading cities of the Roman Empire. After the Emperor Severus divided the province of Britain in two, "Eboracum" was named the capital of Lower Britain.

Severus was one of several Roman Emperors to visit or live in the city. It was his Imperial Court until he died here in 211. Previously Hadrian had used the city as a base for his northern campaigns. In 306 Emperor Constantius Chlorus died at York and was succeeded by his son Constantine. He was proclaimed Emperor while at York and would become Constantine the Great, the first Christian Emperor and founder of Constantinople.

Over 300 years of Roman occupation in York came to an end about 400 when the Roman legions were withdrawn from Britain to serve in Gaul.

¶
Tomb of Lucius Duccius Rufinus, Standard Bearer of the Ninth Legion

· EOFORWIC ·
ANGLO-SAXON YORK

In the fifth century, following the Roman abandonment of Britain, the Germanic tribes of the Anglo Saxons began their long term invasion of the country.

They were met by pockets of fierce resistance, led by local kings and chieftains. The most famous of these was King Arthur who, according to legend, recaptured York from the invaders.

Eventually York would become "Eoforwic," the centre of the independent kingdom of Northumbria, ruled by mighty Anglo-Saxon warlords.

One of these was Edwin, who was instrumental in reintroducing Christianity to Northumbria. He married a Christian princess from the south who brought to York a priest named Paulinus. Paulinus baptised Edwin and many of his subjects on Easter Day 627 in a timber church built especially for the occasion. This was the first cathedral of St. Peter at York and was probably built on the site of the present York Minster. He later became the first bishop of York.

Christianity also brought learning to York. The renowned scholar Alcuin was headmaster of the school of St. Peter at York and received students from all over Europe. He was given the post of Master of Charlemagne's Palace School at Aachen.

¶
The Anglo-Saxon York Helmet at York Castle Museum

By the eighth century "Eoforwic" dominated this part of Britain. But a century later Northumbria was in decline, and in 866 was overrun by Ivar the Boneless and his hordes of Danish Vikings.

Up Helly A' Vikings, at the
Jorvik Viking Festival
¶

· JORVIK ·
—VIKING YORK—

Ivar the Boneless chose an opportune moment for his great invasion. The kingdom of Northumbria was in the midst of a civil war when the Vikings raided and captured York on the first of November 866.

Ten years later the Viking King Halfdan shared out the lands of Northumbria from this capital of "Jorvik" and the warriors settled down to a more peaceful farming existence. "Jorvik" became a major river port, part of the extensive Viking trading routes throughout northern Europe. The city walls were substantially extended and new streets laid down.

The last Viking ruler of York, Eric Bloodaxe, was driven from the city in 954 by King Eadred of Wessex, who succeeded in uniting Northumbria with the southern kingdom. But for another hundred years, Northumbria was still largely ruled by earls of both Anglo and Scandinavian blood.

In the years 1065-66 York changed hands following local rebellion, Norwegian invasion and finally the defeat of the Norwegian army at Stamford Bridge. Three weeks later the victor, King Harold II of England, would fall before the Norman invasion of William the Conqueror at the Battle of Hastings.

9

· NORMAN & MEDIEVAL YORK ·
SECOND CITY OF ENGLAND

William came to York in 1069 to subdue rebellion in the north. He ruthlessly pursued a policy of scorched earth, causing great destruction and poverty from the Ouse to the Tees. To establish his rule he built two wooden castles in York on top of earth mounds, one on each side of the Ouse. These mounds survive today and are at Clifford's Tower and Baile Hill.

William's census of 1086, the Domesday Book, showed that half of York belonged to the King, while the other half was all owned by influential Normans. In time, York began to prosper under William. The rebuilding of the Minster was begun, and before long there were 45 parish churches, 4 monasteries and several religious hospitals in the city. The church exercised tremendous control but later King John granted the city the right to be governed by a Mayor.

Meanwhile, York was once again becoming a profitable port and centre of trade, particularly in wool. A new merchant class was beginning to exercise power. King Henry I granted these leading merchants and craftsmen the city's first charter, confirming their trading rights in England and Normandy. Over a hundred crafts were practised in York in the Middle Ages, presided over by guilds. The wealthiest and most powerful of these was the Merchant Adventurers, the guild of overseas traders. This guild is still active in the city, as are the Merchant Taylors, the Butchers and the guilds of Building, Freemen and Cordwainers.

York grew to become the second largest and richest city in the country and was the northern capital of England. The stone city walls and gates were built during this time. Several Kings and Queens visited

the city, and the Dukedom of York was created, a title often held by the Sovereign's second son.

Henry III's sister and daughter were both married in the Minster to Kings of Scotland. During the reigns of the three Edwards the Departments of State and the Royal Court were moved to York, and Edward III held parliament in York in 1332. Richard II was a regular visitor and he gave the city its first Sword of State and made York a county in its own right. In 1396 the city staged a royal performance of the famous Mystery Plays for Richard III. These have since been revived and are performed in York every four years during the York Festival.

But York's prosperity and special position would not last.

The population was decreasing, the important wool industry was moving elsewhere, and the citizens were soon to take up arms in the Wars of the Roses.

The City of York's
Sword of State

11

· THE AGE OF DECLINE ·

Although the Wars of the Roses between 1453 and 1487 did not have a great economic impact on York, their aftermath did. The self-crowned King Edward IV never forgave York for its Lancastrian sympathies at certain stages during the Wars, and ruled the city harshly. On top of this there followed severe epidemics, the decline of the wool industry, and the shift of much trade away from York to London.

Worse was yet to come. In 1533 Henry VIII renounced Rome, made himself head of the Church of England, and in 1536 began the Dissolution of the Monasteries. York, as a major religious centre, suffered greatly. All the monasteries and friaries were suppressed and their sacred treasures stolen or destroyed. Half of the houses in York, formerly owned by the churches, were seized by the crown and sold to royal officials and London merchants.

Henry did, however, reorganize and strengthen the old Council in the Northern Parts, giving the north more say in its own affairs. The Council took over the Abbot's house at St. Mary's Abbey and renamed it King's Manor. This was the administrative centre of the north and helped York retain its title as the second city of England.

· CIVIL WAR & THE SIEGE · OF YORK

During the 45 year reign of Elizabeth I the Council of the North was further strengthened and York began to revive. The revival continued under James I as York increasingly became a social capital for the gentry of the north. The shops and inns once again flourished and many fine new houses were built.

The boom continued even while Charles I, who came to York in 1639, was King. When Parliament abolished the Northern Council, Charles set up court in the King's Manor, installed the Royal Mint nearby and kept his printing press at St. William's College.

By the time Charles left York in 1642, the Parliamentarian opposition had gathered strength. Civil war erupted and in April 1644 a Parliamentarian army of 40,000 began the Siege of York. At the end of June the siege was lifted when Charles' nephew Prince Rupert arrived with 14,500 troops.

The retreating Parliamentarians were chased to Marston Moor, six miles from York.

The 'Sealed Knot' in action in York
¶

Unfortunately for Rupert, they turned on his army and he was devastatingly defeated. Rupert's army limped back to York and the siege was renewed.

The city surrendered on the 15th of July. Many buildings had been destroyed but further damage was avoided thanks to the Parliamentarian general Sir Thomas Fairfax. As a local man, he respected the conditions of surrender, and prevented his troops from pillaging York's magnificent churches and removing medieval stained glass.

Sir Thomas Fairfax
¶

· GEORGIAN YORK – SOCIAL · CAPITAL OF THE NORTH

Following the removal of the Royal Garrison from York in 1688, the city was gradually dominated by the local aristocracy and gentry. While trade and manufacturing were in decline, York's role as the social and cultural centre for wealthy northerners was on the rise.

Many elegant new townhouses appeared, notably in Micklegate, Blossom Street and Bootham. Public building also enjoyed a boom and included the Assembly Rooms, Assize Courts and Female Prison, as well as numerous hospitals.

Coffeehouses became popular gathering places and so did the new Racecourse. York's first newspaper, the York Mercury, was printed in 1719. Among its population York could now count a growing group of talented writers, artists and craftsmen.

Georgian York saw a great improvement in coach services to and from the city. The former four day journey to London took only 20 hours by the 1830's. And it was soon to take much less time, with the coming of the railway.

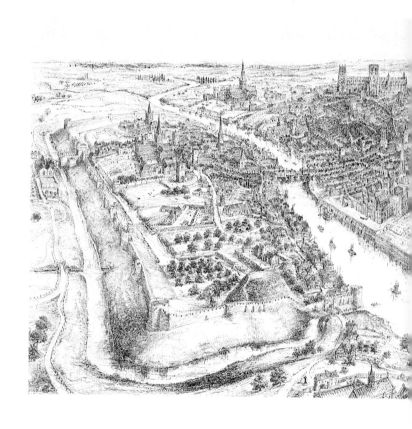

¶
'York in the 15th Century' –
E Ridsdale Tate

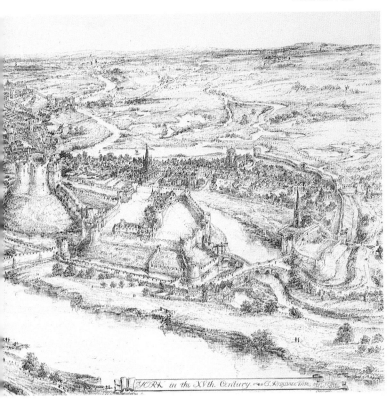

· THE RAILWAY AGE TO ·
THE PRESENT DAY

The man largely responsible for bringing the railway to York in 1839 was an entrepreneur named George Hudson. Ten years later, Hudson's dubious dealings had brought him disgrace. But by this time, York was a major railway centre, and at the turn of the 20th century the railway employed over 5,500 people.

The railway was also instrumental in the expansion of Rowntree's Cocoa Works and Terry's Confectionery Works.

These former small city shops became great factories, and along with the railway, are still York's biggest employers.

In the Victorian era, York witnessed a rapid rise in new church construction, as well as the building of numerous banks, offices, schools and colleges.

In recent years, one of York's most impressive projects was the new University, opened in 1963. During the sixties, it became increasingly obvious that the ancient city was its own major asset, and in 1968 the entire historic core of York was designated a Conservation Area.

Today York is a city which is proud of its past and the role it has played in the nation's history. King George VI said "The history of York is the history of England," and the city's future is just as important. The strength and creativity which have been present for centuries are still being shown by York City Council as it builds towards the 21st century for the people of York and its millions of welcome visitors.

University of York

· FAMOUS YORK PEOPLE ·

· W.H. AUDEN ·

The world famous poet was born in York in 1907 into a family of physicians. His early interest in science put him on his intended path of becoming a mining engineer. But by the age of fifteen he had discovered his poetic nature, and had his first poem published two years later. In 1925 Auden entered Oxford and developed a formidable reputation as a poet and thinker. During the 30's he was a hero of the left and in 1939 he emigrated to the United States and became an American citizen. His prodigious output includes several volumes of poetry, libretti for opera, travel books and criticism. Among Auden's numerous achievements was a Pulitzer Prize, the National Book Award and a professorship at Oxford. The best of Auden's poetry is found in two volumes: Collected Shorter Poems 1927-57 and Collected Longer Poems. Auden died in 1973 in Vienna.

¶
Still from 'The Night Mail,' classic film based on one of Auden's poems

· MARGARET · CLITHEROW

ST. MARGARET OF YORK

Life was difficult and dangerous for Catholics in the latter half of the 16th century. Margaret Clitherow died a horrible death for the crimes of saying mass and offering refuge to priests, when both these activities were illegal. The young butcher's wife refused to testify at her trial and was subjected to a gruesome execution on the 25th March 1586. A door was placed on top of her and piled with heavy stones until she slowly crushed to death. She was canonized in 1970, and her home at No. 35 The Shambles is now a shrine to her memory.

· WILLIAM ETTY ·

This baker's son became York's most famous painter, although at one time he was condemned for 'impropriety and lasciviousness' for his many paintings of nudes. Etty helped to save Bootham Bar from demolition in 1825, he gave generously to the Minster restoration fund after the 1829 fire, and he was an early supporter of the National Gallery. A large collection of Etty's landscapes, portraits and still-lifes are on display at the York City Art Gallery.

'Venus and Cupid' –
William Etty
¶

· GUY FAWKES ·

Perhaps York's most infamous citizen, for his participation in the Gunpowder Plot of 1605, the attempt to blow up the Houses of Parliament. Fawkes was born in what is now Young's Hotel in Petergate and baptized at St. Michael-le-Belfrey, next to York Minster. The church's baptismal register is now in the Minster Library and is open at the entry for Guy Fawkes.

He attended St. Peter's School on Bootham, where he met many of his fellow conspirators. On the 4th of November, Fawkes and the gunpowder were discovered, and he was hung from Traitor's Gate in London three months later. The 5th of November, the day Parliament was supposed to explode, is still celebrated all over England as 'Guy Fawkes Day,' with fireworks, bonfires and the burning of Fawkes in effigy. Everywhere, that is, except at St. Peter's School in York.

· GEORGE HUDSON ·

York's 'Railway King' was three times Mayor of the city, and a self-made millionaire. He was instrumental in bringing the railway to York in 1839 and at one time his railway empire covered a quarter of the British network. Hudson fell from grace in 1849 when financial irregularities were discovered in his business dealings, and he died in relative poverty in 1871. After his fall, the city changed George Hudson Street to Railway Street, but in 1971 he was forgiven, and the street reverted to its original name, in recognition of Hudson's contribution to York. George Hudson's house still stands at No. 44 Monkgate.

· JOSEPH HANSOM ·

Remembered as the inventor of the Hansom Cab, but he made his fortune as a successful architect. Hansom's career was launched in 1831 when his design for the Birmingham Town Hall was chosen in a national competition.

He went on to design grand houses, public schools, halls and churches all over the country, including St. George's Church in York.

Hansom also founded the journal "The Builder," still published today. A fine example of his famous Hansom Cab is on display in "Kirkgate" in the Castle Museum. Hansom was born at 114 Micklegate and the house still stands today.

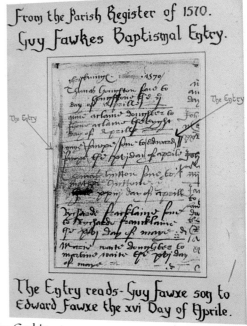

From the Parish Register of 1570.
Guy Fawkes Baptismal Entry.

The Entry reads- Guy Fawxe son to Edward Fawxe the xvi Day of Aprile.

· JONATHAN · MARTIN

On the evening of the 1st February 1829 this religious fanatic started the first and worst York Minster fire. Believing he had been chosen by God to destroy the Minster, Martin set fire to the organ, and before it was discovered the next morning, the entire choir had been devastated. At his trial, Martin was found not guilty by reason of insanity and was committed to Bedlam Hospital in London, where he died nine years later.

· DICK TURPIN ·

A notorious smuggler, poacher and thief whose exploits were greatly romanticised by the 19th century novelist Harrison Ainsworth in his book "Rookwood."

Turpin's criminal career appeared to come to an end when he changed his name and his ways and settled in York as a gentleman.

It didn't last. He was caught stealing a horse. A letter to his brother, demanding an alibi, was intercepted and Turpin's true identity was discovered. He spent three months in the old Debtor's Prison, now part of the Castle Museum, before being hanged on the 7th April 1739.

Cronies took his body to the Blue Boar Inn on Castlegate to cheat the graverobbers, and later buried him in St. George's graveyard.

· GUIDED TOUR ·

The ideal way to see York is on foot. The centre of the ancient walled city is compact, full of history and wonderful surprises, and the towering Minster is a perfect landmark. The Association of Voluntary Guides to the City of York offer an informative guided walking tour. But if you prefer to do the route yourself, at your own pace, just follow the simple instructions below.

¶
Multangular Tower

1. Start at Exhibition Square, outside Bootham Bar, and face the Tourist Information Centre.

2. On your right, there is a lane past the side of King's Manor leading into the Museum Gardens. Follow this lane to the second pathway on the left, which leads to the Anglian and Multangular Towers. The Romans built the Multangular Tower in the 4th century as part of the city's fortifications. As you enter the tower, you face the ruins of St. Leonard's Hospital, dating mainly from the 13th century. The Anglian Tower on the left was built between 600 and 700 A.D. in a breach in the Roman Wall. Remains of Roman, Anglo-Saxon and Medieval walls can be seen here.

3. Return to Museum Gardens and the ruins of the 11th century St. Mary's Abbey, dissolved by Henry VIII in 1539. The famous York Mystery Plays are performed here every four years during the York Festival.

4. Return to Exhibition Square. King's Manor on your left was formerly the house of the Abbot of St. Mary's. Henry VIII made it the headquarters for his King's Council of the North. The house was altered and extended at that time, and is now part of the University of York. The City Art Gallery behind the fountains in the Square was built in 1879 on part of the Abbey grounds, and contains a fine collection of paintings spanning six centuries.

¶
Micklegate Bar

5. Cross the road to Bootham Bar and walk along the walls to Monk Bar. These walls are medieval, dating from the 13th century, and offer excellent views of the Minster, Minster Library and houses and gardens such as Gray's Court.

6. Leave the walls at Monk Bar and walk along Goodramgate. Turn right into Ogleforth, where you can see the courtyard of Gray's Court, and continue left into Chapter House Street. Passing the

Treasurer's House on your right, you arrive at the East End of the Minster and St. William's College. This was the medieval house of the chantry priests of the Minster. Now take College Street back to Goodramgate.

7. Turn right on Goodramgate and walk past the ancient houses of Lady Row to Holy Trinity Church, with its saddleback roof, box pews and 15th century East Window.

8. At the end of Goodramgate turn left into King's Square and the Shambles, medieval street of the butchers. This ends at the Pavement, where you face Sir Thomas Herbert's House, home of the family of powerful Merchant Adventurers of the 16th century. Cross the Pavement, turn right then left on to Piccadilly. A short walk brings you to the entrance to Coppergate, home of the Jorvik Viking Centre and next to it, the York Story, in the former St. Mary's Church. Beside the York Story is Fairfax House. A short walk through the car park brings you to Clifford's Tower, and just beyond, the Castle Museum.

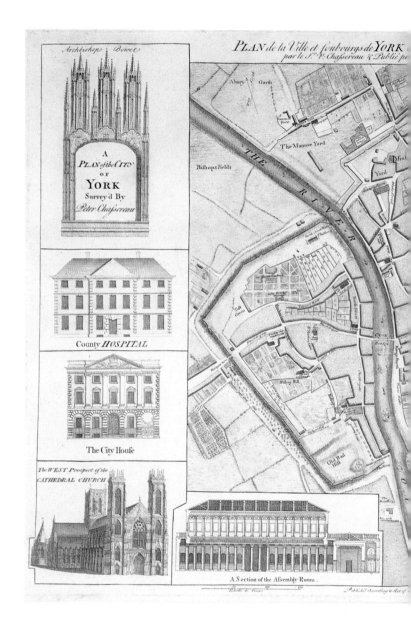

Archbishops Bowet

A
PLAN of the CITY
OF
YORK
Survey'd By
Peter Chassereau

County HOSPITAL

The City House

The WEST Prospect of the
CATHEDRAL CHURCH

PLAN de la Ville et fauxbourgs de YORK
par le Sr. P. Chassereau & Public pe

Almry Garth

The Manner Yard

Bishops Fields

THE RIVER

Mint

Yard

Bishop Hill

OLD Hall

A Section of the Assembly Room.

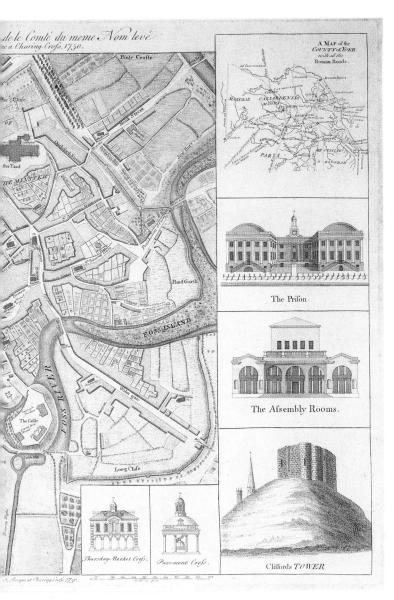

de le Comté du meme Nom levé
se a Charing-Cross, 1750.

Penly Crofs.

Mont Street

Jew Bury

THE MINSTER

St Saviour Gate

Pond Garth

FOSS ISLAND

Walm Gate

FOSS RIVER

The Castle

Castle Mill

Long Clofe

J. Rocque at Charing Crofs 1750.

Scale of Feet

Thursday Market Crofs.

Pavement Crofs.

A MAP of the
COUNTY of YORK
with all the
Roman Roads.

EBORACUM

PARIS

The Prifon

The Afsembly Rooms.

Cliffords TOWER

'A Plan of the City of York,
1750' – John Rocque after
Peter Chassereau

¶

23

· YORK MINSTER ·

York Minster's official name is the Cathedral and Metropolitical Church of St. Peter. It is the Mother Church of the Northern Province of the Church of England, with the Archbishop of York as its Primate. And it is both a Cathedral and a Minster. A Cathedral because it is a church with a bishop's or archbishop's throne, and a Minster because it was in Saxon times, as now, served by a team of clergy.

York Minster is the largest Gothic church in England. This vast and lofty building measures 534 ft (160 m) long and 249 ft (76 m) wide across the transepts. The height from floor to vault is over 90 ft (27 m), the twin west towers are about 184 ft (65 m) high and the lantern tower higher still.

¶
Great East Window

· HISTORY ·

THE ROMAN · PRINCIPIA ·

This has always been the site of York's most important building. In the Roman Age, the principia or military headquarters stood here. Important relics of that era are displayed in the Minster's Undercroft Museum, where you can also trace the actual foundations of the Roman building.

'South West prospect of York Minster, 1750' – François Vivares after Joseph Baker
¶

· THE FIRST MINSTER ·

Even in Roman times there was a Christian Bishop of York. But after the legions withdrew, Britain reverted to pagan beliefs under Anglo-Saxon invaders.

Kent had become a Christian kingdom again by 625, when Princess Ethelburga came north to marry King Edwin of Northumbria, who was still pagan. She brought her chaplain Paulinus, so she could still worship as a Christian, and within two years they had persuaded Edwin to be baptised.

The ceremony took place on Easter Day 627 here in his capital city of York, then called "Eoforwic." The little wooden church that was built for the rite was the first York Minster, and Paulinus was its first Bishop.

After his baptism, Edwin began to build a stone church, but in 633 he was killed in battle and his church was completed, then fell into disrepair. It was largely rebuilt in 670 by the then bishop of York, St. Wilfred. This rebuilt church served York until after the Norman Conquest.

· THE NORMAN CATHEDRALS ·

The first Norman cathedral was built between 1080 and 1100. The extent of its great eastern apse can still be traced in the present crypt and considerable remains of its walls can be seen in the Undercroft. Between 1160 and 1170, the eastern arm was enlarged and altered by Archbishop Roger. Re-used carved capitals and pillars from this period can be seen in the crypt. In the western crypt Archbishop Roger's work may be seen in situ.

¶
View from South East

· THE GOTHIC CATHEDRAL ·

The south and north transepts were built in the Early English style between 1215 and 1260. During the next 25 years the lovely octagonal Chapter House was completed in the Decorated Style, the second stage of Gothic architecture.

The nave, built between 1291 and 1350 is also Decorated, but the choir, which followed between 1361 and 1450, is in the Perpendicular style. The twin west towers were completed by 1472, and the massive central lantern tower by 1480. The cathedral had taken over 250 years to build.

STAINED · GLASS ·

The stained glass of York Minster is one of its greatest treasures; nowhere else in England can so much medieval glass be seen in one church.

'Interior Scaffolding, west end Minster' – Joseph Halfpenny
¶

There is some modern glass, too, so that the whole field of glass painting from the 12th to the 20th centuries is represented.

At the beginning of World War Two about 80 of the finest windows were taken out for safety. The windows were cleaned and restored and by the time they were replaced they had been brought back to their former glory. The restoration project took over twenty years.

· THE BECKWITH/NOLLOTH BELLS ·

In 1840 the former bells were destroyed by fire. The present bells were the replacement and are sometimes known as the Beckwith peal as they were purchased with £2000 left to the Minster by a York physician, Dr Stephen Beckwith.

All the bells were recast in 1925-27 and a new bell added under the direction of, and largely paid for by, Canon H E Nolloth. Before Dr. Beckwith's gift became known, an appeal had been launched for new bells and money poured in from all over the world. Big Peter, the principal bell of the Minster, was purchased with these donations.

The eleven ton bell arrived from London on the "new" railway in 1845. The fanfare subsided when it was discovered that the bell had a casting fault and did not match the peal in tone. For 80 years it was used only on solemn occasions, and to mark the hours of midday and midnight.

Then, in 1927, Big Peter was recast and it is now the deepest toned bell in Europe. Its rich and sonorous tone is a perfect complement to the peal. Big Peter now proudly rings every day at noon; the whole peal on Sundays, practice nights and for special events.

· MONUMENTAL BRASSES ·

Notable brasses in the Minster include Archbishop Wm. Grenefield, 1315; Eliz. Eynns, 1585; and Jas. Cotrel, 1595. Brass rubbing is no longer allowed in the Minster.

· FIRES ·

The Minster suffered two disastrous fires in the 19th century.
In February 1829, a fanatic named Jonathan Martin set fire to the choir stalls and the choir was completely burnt out. Only two of the 15th century canopied stalls were not totally destroyed.

The second fire happened in 1840 when a careless workman left a candle burning in the south-west tower. The tower burned, the bells crashed to the ground, and the nave suffered severe damage.

The fires caused even more damage because the centre vault of the Minster in both the choir and nave is made of timber, and was destroyed each time.

The latest fire at the Minster happened during a freak summer storm in 1984. Lightning was the most likely cause and the whole roof of the south transept was consumed by flames. Miraculously there was very little other damage. The task of replacing the outer roof was finished in 1986, and the complicated inner vault with its 68 carved bosses is expected to be ready in 1988.

¶
'The Burning of York Minster' as it appeared from the City Walls, May 20 1840

· RESTORATION ·

A massive restoration job was undertaken at the Minster between 1967 and 1972. Uneven settling had caused serious cracks in the central lantern tower, the east end was leaning outwards over 2 feet and the west towers were also unstable. New foundations of reinforced concrete were constructed under these areas, and danger spots in other parts of the building were also made safe. Valuable historic finds were discovered during the concurrent archaeological excavations and are now contained in the Undercroft Museum.

· TOUR OF THE MINSTER ·

1
· THE SOUTH TRANSEPT ·
Mainly Early English architecture, featuring the long, simple lancet windows of the first Gothic period. Built between 1220 and 1240. Now temporarily closed until 1988, due to fire restoration work.

2
· ROSE WINDOW ·
This famous window commemorates the 1486 marriage of King Henry VII and Elizabeth of York, which ended the Wars of the Roses and began the Tudor dynasty. The glass dates from the early 16th century, but the central "sunflower" is 18th century.

¶
Rose Window

3
· THE DE GREY TOMB ·
Archbishop Walter de Grey was buried in the south transept in 1255. During restoration of his canopied tomb, a painting of him was discovered below the marble effigy, and inside the coffin were his chalice, paten, cross and ring. These are now on display in the Undercroft.

4
· THE NAVE ·
Built in the Decorated style between 1291 and about 1350.

5
· GREAT WEST WINDOW ·
The finest of many 14th century windows in the nave, dating from 1338. The tracery is in the form of a heart and is often called the "Heart of Yorkshire." Unfortunately, the window tracery has crumbled so badly it is being replaced. Some of the famous glass will be on display in the Undercroft during 1987.

¶
The Nave

6
· ST. PETER ·
This figure of the Minster's patron saint stands between the great west doors. Below, on the temporary panelling, are lists of the Bishops and Archbishops of York, Deans of York and other major dignitaries of the Chapter.

7
· ST. CUTHBERT'S CHAPEL ·
The Regimental Chapel of the Yorkshire Volunteers, dedicated in 1982.

8
· THE NORTH TRANSEPT ·
Built between 1241 and 1260 in the Early English style.

Five Sisters Window
¶

9
· ST. JOHN'S CHAPEL ·
Regimental Chapel of the King's Own Yorkshire Light Infantry.

10
· FIVE SISTERS WINDOW ·
These five giant lancets are each over 50 ft (15 m) tall and more than 5 ft (1.5 m) wide, and date from the 13th century. It was the inspiration for Charles Dickens' story about five York sisters who worked lengths of tapestry, and had them copied in stained glass as a memorial when the youngest sister died.

11
· THE CHAPTER HOUSE ·
The Chapter House was built in the Decorated style between 1260 and 1285, and is entered by way of the vestibule. The building is regarded as an architectural wonder. Despite its colossal size and the weight of its conical roof, there is no central pillar to lessen the downward and outward thrust onto the buttresses and walls.

12
· ASTRONOMICAL CLOCK ·
This is a memorial to 18,000 airmen of the R.A.F. and other air forces who were stationed in the north-east and lost their lives in World War Two.

13
· TOMB OF ·
ARCHBISHOP Wm. DE GRENEFIELD
(d. 1316) On top of this is one of the few brasses in existence from this period.

14
· STRIKING CLOCK ·
The clock on the east wall has two medieval figures, Gog and Magog, which strike the quarter hours.

¶
Chapter House Roof

· THE CROSSING AND LANTERN TOWER ·

From the crossing between the transepts it is possible to look up into the lantern tower to the distant vaulted roof. The great central boss shows St. Peter holding the Church and the Keys of Heaven, and St. Paul with the Gospels and a sword.

16

· CHOIR SCREEN ·

The 15th century stone screen between the choir and nave depicts the Kings of England from William I to Henry VI. Above the kings is a canopy of angels all playing different musical instruments to the glory of God Father, who is enthroned above the central arch. This splendid arch forms the western entrance to the choir; its vaulted roof has a superb boss of the Assumption of the Virgin.

¶
'York Cathedral, The Choir, c 1840' – Francis Bedford

17
· THE CHOIR ·
Built between 1361 and 1450 in the Perpendicular style.

18
ARCH-
· BISHOP'S ·
THRONE
In the middle of the choir on the south side is the throne of the Archbishop of York. It is this throne which gives the Minster the status of a cathedral; "cathedra" is the Latin word for a throne.

19
CHOIR
· STALLS ·
These stalls were built in the 19th century to replace the 15th century stalls destroyed in the 1829 fire. The four at the west end, two each side of the entrance, are for the Dean, Precentor, Chancellor and Treasurer; the rest are for the non-residentiary Canons and other officials.

· HIGH ALTAR ·

Erected in its present form in the 20th century. The main daily services are sung in the choir.

2 1

· THE NORTH CHOIR AISLE ·

Interesting monuments include those to Prince William of Hatfield; Archbishop Richard Sterne; and Sir Henry Bellasis, his wife Ursula and their three children.

2 2

TOMB OF PRINCE WILLIAM · OF · HATFIELD

William was the second son of Edward III, and was only 8 years old when he died. The only Royal tomb in the Minster.

Choir Screen
¶

2 3

· THE ST. WILLIAM WINDOW ·

A giant window in the so-called "north-east transept" depicting the life of this saint.

2 4

· ST. STEPHEN'S CHAPEL ·

The terra cotta relief behind the altar is a fine representation of a Crucifixion and dates from the mid-19th century.

2 5

· THE LADY CHAPEL ·

This is the chapel behind the high altar.

2 6

· NATIVITY REREDOS ·

The carved panelling on the east wall commemorates Queen Victoria's Diamond Jubilee and shows both the Adoration of the Shepherds and the Visit of the Magi.

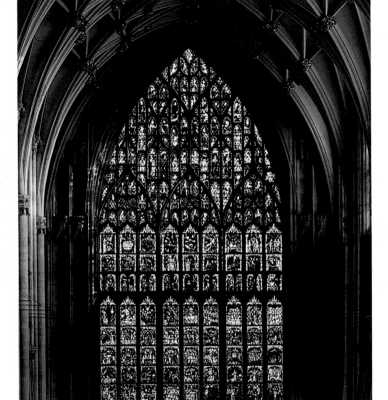

Great East Window

¶

27
THE GREAT · EAST · WINDOW

One of the Minster's greatest treasures, created between 1405 and 1408. In the apex is God the Father. The open book in front of him reads 'Ego Sum Alpha et Omega' – 'I am the Beginning and the End.' This is the theme of the window. The panels show the Beginning from Creation to the End, from the Revelation of St. John the Divine.

28
· STALLS ·

(against the stone screen) Modern stalls by Thompson of Kilburn with his famous mouse trademark.

29
ALL · SAINTS' · CHAPEL

The Regimental Chapel of the Duke of Wellington's Regiment, commemorating the men who fell in the First World War.

30
· THE SOUTH CHOIR AISLE ·

The modern paintings on the screen between choir and aisle are memorials to architects and healers. The elaborate monuments include those to Archbishop Lamplugh, wearing the mitre and carrying his staff, and Archbishop John Dolben, who was severely wounded at the Battle of Marston Moor, before taking holy orders.

· THE CRYPT ·

Ask a guide to take you in. The Altars are dedicated to St. Edwin, St. Paulinus and St. Hilda. Between them is a much mutilated 12th century carving of the Madonna and Child, and a medieval carving of St. Anne teaching the Child Virgin to read. Below a trapdoor is the base of a Roman Pillar (dating from about A.D. 300) and probably belonging to the legionary commander's house. The markings on the floor forming semicircles show the extent of foundation of the Norman eastern apse. The Doomstone is a Norman carving, depicting Hell as a cauldron, with wicked souls being led in. The Font cover commemorates the baptism of King Edwin of Northumbria in 627.

32

· THE ST. CUTHBERT WINDOW ·

Depicts the life of St. Cuthbert and is a twin of the St. William window.

33

· THE ZOUCHE CHAPEL ·

This small chapel is set aside for private prayer, although services are held here as well. The only two 15th century choir stalls to survive the fire of 1829 are located here.

34

· THE UNDERCROFT MUSEUM ·

This unique museum was created as a result of unexpected finds made during the Minster's restoration of 1967-72. The history of York and its Minster is traced among the remains of the ancient Roman principia and early Cathedrals built on this site.

Items on display include Saxon tombstones and stone carvings, fine Roman painted wall plaster and many other finds from the archaeological excavations.

In the Treasury, some of the Minster's finest treasures are on display: the Horn of Ulf, given to the Minster by a relative of King Canute; a 13th century Heart Casket, which probably belonged to a Crusader; personal treasures from Archbishop de Grey's tomb; and a fine collection of York silver.

¶
Undercroft Museum

35

· ST. GEORGE'S CHAPEL ·

This is the chapel of the West Yorkshire Regiment, where colours are laid up and memorial books housed. Their famous battles are named on the railings.

36

ENTRANCE TO CENTRAL · TOWER ROOF ·

275 steps take you up to York's highest point, with magnificent views and fascinating close-ups of curious stone carvings.

37

· MINSTER BOOKSHOP ·

Offers a wide range of books about the Minster, guides, postcards, and many other items.

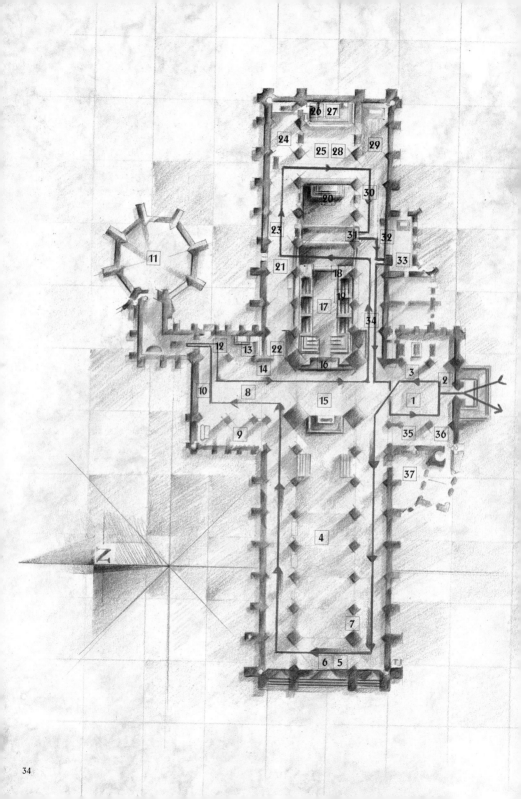

· A WALK AROUND ·
THE MINSTER

On leaving the Minster by the West Door, look up to the twin bell towers, each topped with eight slender finger pinnacles nearly 30 ft (10 m) high. The Beckwith peal hangs in the south-west tower, the 11-ton Big Peter in the north-west.

Turning right from the west front, the entrance to Dean's Park leads to the north side of the nave, with its row of 20th Century flying buttresses, and then to the long lancet windows of the north transept. Next is the conical-roofed Chapter House, with massive buttresses at every angle. Further on at the east end there is a fine view of the Great East Window. The row of stone heads beneath includes Christ and the Twelve Apostles.

Turn right again, to the south choir aisle, then again to the south entrance. Now walk the length of the nave. Notice how carved heads, figures and pinnacles decorate the building to a great height. Continue on until you return to the West Door.

Finger Pinnacles
¶

· FLOODLIGHTING ·

The Minster dominates the city by night as well as by day. Both the east and west fronts and lantern tower are brilliantly floodlit from dusk, making the Minster visible from every direction.

· CITY WALLS ·

· ROMAN WALL ·

The first wall was a simple earth and wood stockade built by the Romans to surround their early fort. The Ninth Legion added stone walls in the second century, which enclosed a much smaller area than the present walled city; only about 50 acres then, compared to 260 acres now.

From the Multangular Tower the Roman Wall roughly followed the present medieval wall through Bootham Bar to the northern corner tower, then continued on by Monk Bar to a point behind Merchant Taylors' Hall. The Roman wall then turned south-west to King's Square, where there was a gateway, and continued on to a corner tower at what is now Feasegate. From here, the wall turned north-west to the Roman's Praetorian Gate, which stood at St. Helen's Square, then continued along to the Multangular Tower.

· MEDIEVAL WALL ·

The wall you walk on today is the medieval wall, almost three miles around. It dates from the 13th century and stands on an earth rampart built by the Anglo-Danish Kings of York, and later enlarged by the Normans. The wall has been extensively restored in the last two centuries.

· POINTS OF INTEREST ·

—————— 1 ——————
· LENDAL TOWER ·

Start here and, with the river on your left, walk clockwise. This riverside defensive tower was extensively rebuilt in the 19th century. A chain was stretched from here, across the river to the North Street Postern Tower, to prevent enemy ships sailing into the city. From 1677 to 1836 Lendal Tower housed the pumping engine that supplied York with water.

¶
Lendal Tower

2

· WALL FROM ST. LEONARD'S · HOSPITAL TO MULTANGULAR TOWER

Medieval superstructure on Roman base. By St. Leonard's Hospital, on the Museum Gardens side, is the base of a Roman interval tower.
The hole in the wall nearest the Multangular Tower, now patched with larger stones, was made during the Siege of York in 1644. The little circular brick floor just inside the wall at this point is the base of a Roman kiln.

¶ Multangular Tower

3
· MULTANGULAR TOWER ·

The west corner tower of Roman York and the oldest part of the city. The wall here is Roman to a height of 19 ft (6.2 m), though the exterior has been repaired with modern masonry.
The upper part, of larger stones, is medieval.
The Roman coffins inside the tower were unearthed from various sites in York.

4
· WALL FROM MULTANGULAR · TOWER TO EXHIBITION SQUARE

Medieval wall built outside the line of the Roman wall. The gap to Bootham Bar was cut in the 1830's to build St. Leonard's Place and is the only major breach in the walls. The Roman wall here leads northwards from the Multangular Tower to the Anglian Tower.

5
· ANGLIAN TOWER ·

This is the only remaining part of the city's defensive stonework built between the departure of the Romans and medieval times. Note how crude it is compared to the Roman work.

¶ Bootham Bar

6
· FRAGMENT · OF ROMAN WALL

In car park of St. Leonard's.

7
· BOOTHAM BAR ·

Here the wall of St. Mary's Abbey joined the city wall at right angles. The Bar incorporates an early Norman outer archway, and is also the only gate on the site of an earlier Roman gate. From here you can walk on top of the wall.

8

· WALL FROM BOOTHAM BAR TO · MONK BAR

Considerably wider than in medieval days and offering wonderful views of the Minster. The best remaining portion of the moat lies between the wall and Lord Mayor's Walk.

9
· MONK BAR ·

The walk does not go through the building, you have to go down to the road and up again. This is the finest of the medieval gates and is vaulted on three floors. It still has a working portcullis, a massive gate that can be lowered to block the road. The carved men holding stones to drop on the enemy's head give the impression of a more powerful defence.

'Layerthorpe Postern, 1907'–
Joseph Halfpenny
¶

10
· MONK BAR TO LAYERTHORPE BRIDGE ·

Pass the remains of the Roman Corner Tower. The gap between Layerthorpe Bridge and the Red Tower was originally marshland and later the King's Fishpool. No wall was ever built on this stretch.

11
· ROMAN CORNER TOWER ·

This tower and stretch of wall is behind Merchant Taylors' Hall. Access is from Goodramgate near Monk Bar. The tower was excavated in 1925-26 and is complete to its full height. The sloping stones on top were originally surmounted by a wooden palisade.

12
· RED TOWER ·

The only substantial brick-built part of the wall. Erected in 1490, but much restored.

13
· WALMGATE BAR ·

The only town gate in England to still have its barbican, an outward extension with an outer gateway. Attackers would have to pass through a narrow funnel under a hail of missiles. Also intact are the wooden doors, portcullis and Elizabethan house on top.

14
· FISHERGATE BAR ·
A minor gateway still with portcullis grooves.

15
· FISHERGATE POSTERN TOWER ·
Built on the original riverbank in 1505, when the Foss was wider. Another fine view of the Minster.

16
· YORK CASTLE ·
Between the Foss and the Ouse the Castle protected the city, and part of its outer wall remains behind the Castle Museum.

17
· STRETCH OF CITY WALL ·
Protected the gap between the Castle and the Ouse. Runs from Tower Street along the edge of St. George's Gardens to Davy Tower on the river bank.

18
· BAILE HILL ·
An artificial mound built by William the Conqueror and originally topped by a wooden castle.

¶
Micklegate Bar

19
· BITCHDAUGHTER TOWER ·
Built between 1317 and 1340. The origins of the Tower's name remain obscure, although it was sited in an area earlier known as Bitchill.

20
· VICTORIA BAR ·
19th century gateway.

21
· MICKLEGATE BAR ·
Kings passed under its fine Norman archway, and traitors' severed heads were displayed on top.

22
· TOFT TOWER ·
A corner tower with an excellent view of the Minster. Down below, in front of the Royal York Hotel, is the Cholera Burial Ground, containing victims of York's last epidemic in July 1832.

23
· NORTH STREET POSTERN · TOWER
The steps beside this tower led to the ferry which crossed here before Lendal Bridge was built.

¶
'All Saint's Church,
Pavement, York 1836' –
W Walton

· THE STREETS OF YORK ·

The streets of York developed from the early Roman fortress, Petergate and Stonegate forming the principal routes within the Garrison.

The Vikings left a lasting mark on York street names with the ending 'gate,' a Scandinavian word for street. Medieval citizens left winding streets and timber-framed houses; the Georgians tall, elegant facades; and the Victorians left many red brick buildings with an abundance of heavy, elaborate ornamentation.

· THE · MAIN STREETS

Bootham is the main road northwards from Bootham Bar. Its name is said to come from the market stalls, or booths, which stood below the walls of St. Mary's Abbey. St. Leonard's Place was created in the 1830's and includes the elegant De Grey Rooms.

On Castlegate, Fairfax House is one of the finest Georgian townhouses in England, and has a superb collection of English furniture. Number 20 was the book publishing house of William Alexander, who turned down Walter Scott's "Ivanhoe" as being 'too frivolous.' Dick Turpin's cronies took his corpse to the Blue Boar Inn to cheat graverobbers, then reburied it at St. George's Churchyard.

¶
Fairfax House

Coney Street is now one of York's main shopping streets, with few remaining old buildings. The name originally meant King's Highway. Note the great clock outside the church of St. Martin-le-Grand.

Fossgate is the home of the Merchant Adventurers' Hall, with its fine coat of arms at the entrance. Across the humpback bridge over the Foss is Dorothy Wilson's Hospital, from the Georgian period.

Goodramgate is said to be named after Gutherum, a Danish chieftain. The many attractive medieval buildings include 14th century Lady Row outside Holy Trinity Church, the oldest row of cottages in York. Goodramgate stretches from Petergate, past the junction with Deangate and turns right to Monk Bar.

Several interesting streets run off this last section of Goodramgate. College Street, occupied mainly by St. William's College. Bedern, with Bedern Hall of 1252, formerly the Chapel of Vicars-Choral, now the home of the Guild of Freemen, Guild of Builders and the Company of Cordwainers. Ogleforth, leading to Gray's Court and pretty, cobbled Chapter House Street. And Aldwark, the address of the Merchant Taylors' Hall. Beyond Monk Bar the fine houses of Monkgate include No. 44, George Hudson's house.

Lady Row Cottages

¶

King's Square was the site of a Roman Gate, and Christ Church stood here until 1937. Its tombstones are still part of the paving.

Micklegate. The name means Great Street, and it is still one of York's main thoroughfares. The many fine Georgian houses date from York's days as the northern social capital. The Railway King Hotel was one of the first railway contractors' offices. Charles Dickens' brother Alfred worked there and was occasionally visited by the novelist. No. 114 was the birthplace of Joseph Hansom, inventor of the Hansom cab.

Micklegate has three historic churches: Holy Trinity at the top, with its stocks in front; St. Martin-cum-Gregory halfway up the hill; and St. John the Evangelist, now the York Arts Centre, at the foot. At the head of the street is Micklegate Bar and beyond is Blossom Street, also with a number of Georgian buildings, including the Bar Convent of about 1760.

North Street features the smallest house in England, beside All Saints Church.

¶

Micklegate

43

<u>The Pavement</u>. This was one of York's first paved streets. The Herbert House of 1557 is a particular fine half-timbered building. Sir Thomas Herbert was given the watch of Charles I as they walked together to the King's execution. Beside this house, a passage leads to <u>Lady Peckett's Yard</u>, a quaint old alley where the ancient houses on each side overhang even closer than in the Shambles. Political prisoners were executed in the Pavement, and stocks and pillories stood here. Between the Pavement and its northern extension, Stonebow, stands Whip-ma-Whop-ma-Gate, York's shortest street. The name may have been derived from the whipping of petty criminals here.

<u>Petergate</u> was the main cross street of Roman York. High Petergate runs from Bootham Bar to <u>Stonegate</u>; from here to <u>King's Square</u> is <u>Low Petergate</u>. This narrow street has a number of interesting buildings of all ages. Nos. 12-18 form an especially nice half-timbered house. Opposite Stonegate is <u>Minster Gates</u>, a short foot passage between Petergate and the Minster. The figure above the Alpha Nova Shop on the corner is Minerva, Goddess of Wisdom, a reminder of the days when this was the street of booksellers. Petergate also has a number of plaques known as 'firemarks.' 18th and 19th century insurance companies had their own private fire brigades, and these plaques identified the properties they insured.

<u>St. Helen's Square</u>, the centre of modern York, was the site of the main Roman entrance to York, the Praetorian Gate. This was also the location of the graveyard for St. Helen's Church, until it was moved in 1745.

<u>St. Saviourgate</u>. A quiet, attractive street, containing the Unitarian Chapel of 1692; St. Saviour's Church, and the great Centenary Methodist Church of 1839-40.

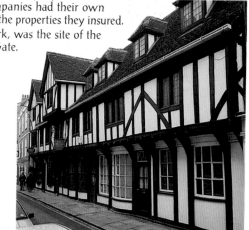

¶
Low Petergate

The Shambles. One of the best preserved medieval streets in Europe. Formerly Fleshammels, the street of the butchers. The shelves in front of the shop windows and the hooks above were for displaying meat. Butcher's Hall is still at No. 40. No. 35 was the house of St. Margaret of York and is now a chapel to her memory. Little Shambles and other streets and alleys lead to Newgate Market, where goods of every kind have been sold for centuries, and still are today. A number of medieval houses surround the market.

Stonegate. One of the finest steets in England, originally the Via Praetoria of Roman York. Mulberry Hall at Nos. 17-19 dates from 1434. Ye Olde Starre Inne is York's oldest recorded ale house. No. 33 was a printer's and the red devil squatting under the eaves is a reminder of "printer's devils," who used to carry the type. The upper stories of this house are dated 1489. Beside it, Coffee Yard is a little alley typical of old York. The Bible over the door at No. 35 shows that this was once a bookshop. At No. 52A is a passage leading to Twelfth Century House. The shop fronts at Nos. 37, 46 and 49 are particularly interesting. Today, Stonegate is famous for its fashion, porcelain and fine art shops.

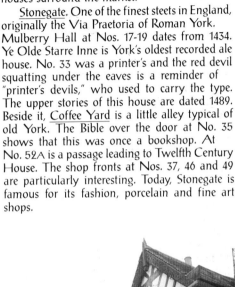

¶
Stonegate

· HISTORIC BUILDINGS ·

· ASSEMBLY ROOMS ·

The Assembly Rooms were built by public subscription between 1732 and 1736. They were a fashionable centre of Georgian York, where great balls and assemblies were held. After World War Two the Rooms were restored and are once again being used for dances, as well as for exhibitions and conferences. Admission free. C3

· THE BLACK SWAN INN ·

The Black Swan, Peasholme Green, was once the home of Martin Bowes, goldsmith to Queen Elizabeth and twice Lord Mayor of London. Sir Martin presented the Sword of State to the city, which is still borne before the Lord Mayor when he goes to the monthly Council Meeting in the Guildhall. Open during normal licensing hours. F3

· CLIFFORD'S TOWER ·

Built on an artificial mound erected by William the Conqueror. His original wooden castle was destroyed by fire during anti-Jewish riots in 1190. 150 Jews took their own lives here, rather than surrender to the mob. The existing stone tower was built in the 13th century. E5

CROWN · COURTS ·

John Carr designed the Crown Courts in 1777 and the Female Prison directly opposite in 1780. The facades are almost identical, but the Crown Courts have more decoration, including the symbols of Law in the pediment and above it, the figure of Justice, with scales and sword. The great grass circle between the two buildings is known as the Eye of York.

Official Proclamations by the High Sheriff of Yorkshire are made on the forecourt. E5

· FAIRFAX HOUSE ·

This outstanding townhouse is a home for a unique collection of Georgian furniture, clocks, paintings and porcelain. The 18th century elegance of York can be enjoyed in the superbly decorated interior, described as a classical architectural masterpiece of its age.

Now owned by the York Civic Trust, and fully restored by them, the remarkable furniture and furnishings enhance and complement the excellence of the house itself.

On Castlegate. Open March 1st - January 1st. E4/5

· GUILDHALL ·

Located behind the Mansion House, the Guildhall is the administrative headquarters of the city. A restoration of the 15th century Commonhall, the building was almost totally destroyed by an air raid in 1942.

¶
Guildhall

The wonderful coloured bosses and grotesques in the wooden roof are copies of the originals. The window above the dais tells the story of York in modern stained glass.

The adjoining Inner Chamber, now a committee room, escaped destruction in 1942.

This room has two secret doorways in the panelling, and still has original bosses and grotesques. The Victorian high Gothic Council Chamber is also well worth a visit. C3

· JUDGES LODGING ·

Used from 1806 to 1976 as a residence for the Judges of Assize during their regular visits to York. Now a hotel with public bar and restaurant. C3

· KING'S MANOR ·

The original building was the home of the Abbot of St. Mary's Abbey. At the Dissolution of the Monasteries it was assigned by Henry VIII as the official residence of the King's Council of the North, and the house was largely rebuilt and surrounded by new apartments. James I and Charles I both stayed here. James' initials I.R. are at the foot of the front doorways, and Charles' initials C.R. are in the Royal Arms over the main doorway.

The King's Council of the North was abolished in 1641, and after the Civil War the house served a variety of uses. It was splendidly restored in 1964 to become part of the University of York. Admission free. C2

THE MANSION · HOUSE ·

Mansion House
¶

Built in 1725-30 to be the official home of the Lord Mayor during his term of office.

Today it is the only "city hall" in England which is purely the private home of the Lord Mayor and his Lady during their term of office.

Not normally open to the public. However, visits may be arranged by prior application to the Lord Mayor's Personal Assistant, The Guildhall, York YO1 1QL. C3

MERCHANT ADVENTURERS' · HALL ·

Dating from the late 14th century, this is one of the few remaining Medieval Guild Halls. Its Great Hall is the largest timber framed building in York. For nearly 600 years the Company controlled the trade of "goods bought and sold foreign" in the city, and was the most powerful and wealthy Company in the city. The Company continues today and the Hall contains many colourful banners of York's Medieval Guilds.

E4

Merchant Adventurers' Hall
¶

· MERCHANT · TAYLORS' HALL

Built by the Confraternity of St. John the Baptist, with panelled walls and a fine 14th century timbered roof. Since the 15th century it has been the hall of the Company of Merchant Taylors.

Open May to September, when no functions are in progress. E2

· MINSTER · LIBRARY

Since 1810 the Minster Library has been in the 13th century chapel of the Archbishop's Palace. The Library is now administered jointly with the University of York and contains a great number of ancient books and manuscripts, many of which can be inspected by visitors. A permanent exhibition of its chief treasures is on view in the upper hall, including illuminated manuscripts and the baptismal register of St. Michael-le-Belfrey church, open at the entry for Guy Fawkes. Admission free. D1

· ROMAN BATH INN ·

At the Roman Bath Inn are the remains of Roman steam baths, including part of the hypocaust, or brick hot-air ducting. This is one of the very few Roman baths ever to be found within a fortress area.

Open during normal licensing hours. D3

· ST. ANTHONY'S HALL ·

Dates from the 15th century. The ancient Guild of St. Anthony was housed here until it was dissolved in 1627. The Hall served a variety of uses until it became the York Blue Coat School in 1705. Today, it is home of the Borthwick Institute, part of the University of York.

Admission free. E/F3

· ST. LEONARD'S HOSPITAL ·

The remains of this rich medieval hospital include the great tunnel-like round arch which was its watergate, the remains of a chapel above, and an undercroft with 13th century vaulting. The original hospital, founded soon after the Norman conquest, was attached to the Minster and dedicated to St. Peter. After a fire in 1137, it was rebuilt and enlarged, and the dedication changed to St. Leonard. Beside the hospital there was a "Bairns' House" or ophanage. The Hospital was suppressed by Henry VIII, and part of its buildings were used for a Royal Mint until 1697.

Admission free. C2

¶
'St Mary's Abbey, York, 1843' – George Hawkins after William Richardson

ST. ·MARY'S· ABBEY

Founded in 1080 and later enlarged, this was once the most important Benedictine monastery in the north of England.

Only foundations of the Norman buildings still exist. Most of the remains in the Museum Gardens and beyond are later medieval, including the ruins of the imposing church, the gatehouse

by the entrance at Marygate, the Hospitium near the river, where the Abbot entertained his guests, and the watergate. The Abbot's House is now part of King's Manor. Many interesting remains of the Abbey are preserved in the Yorkshire Museum.

Free Admission to St. Mary's Abbey. B2

· ST. WILLIAM'S COLLEGE ·

Built in 1453 for Minster Chantry priests, it passed into private hands after the Dissolution of the Monasteries. Charles I had his printing press and Royal Mint here during the Civil War. Later it was divided into tenement dwellings, but was restored in the 1900's to become the meeting place of the Northern Convocation of the Church of England and is now used for meetings of all kinds. E 2

¶
St. William's College

· THEATRE ROYAL ·

Opened in 1740, it became one of the chief Georgian theatres in the country, and was granted the royal patent in 1769. The theatre was extensively rebuilt in Victorian times, and enlarged and modernised in 1967.

Restaurant, bar and coffee bar open during normal hours. Admission to the auditorium only during performances. C 2

· TREASURER'S HOUSE & · GRAY'S COURT

This was the home of the Treasurers of the Minster until that office was dissolved in 1547. After the Dissolution of the Monasteries, the house eventually passed into private hands, and extensive alterations were made. In 1720 the house was divided, and the part known as Gray's Court is today part of the College of Ripon and York St. John.

The Prince and Princess of Wales, later King Edward VII and Queen Alexandra, stayed at Treasurer's House in 1900. The last private owner gave the House and its period furniture to the National Trust in 1930. D 1 / 2

TWELFTH CENTURY · HOUSE ·

This restored remnant of a Norman house stands behind Stonegate and is reached through a narrow passage. The house contains a Norman window and stone-faced wall, the oldest substantial traces of a Norman house in York. Admission free. C 3 / D 2

Treasurer's House

¶

· YORK AT NIGHT ·

Much of York is now floodlit after dark, including the Minster, Guildhall, Mansion House, Art Gallery and King's Manor, Clifford's Tower, Lendal Tower and Bridge, Holy Trinity on Goodramgate, St. Martin-le-Grand, the four great Bars and parts of the city walls.

· THE ANCIENT · CHURCHES

In medieval times there were at least fifty parish churches in York. Eighteen of these remain today, but many are no longer regularly used for worship.

Several of the churches listed here contain monumental brasses, but rubbings are not normally allowed. There is, however, a Brass Rubbing Centre at St. William's College. Replica brasses, moulded by specialists from originals in Yorkshire churches, are available for rubbings. A fee is charged.

· ALL SAINTS ·
NORTH STREET

The slender tower is a riverside landmark between the Ouse and Lendal Bridges. The core is late Norman and the tower is 15th century. In the north-east window, 14th century glass shows scenes from the life of the Virgin Mary. Two superb 15th century windows in the north wall depict the Six Corporal Acts of Mercy and the Last Fifteen Days of the World. The 15th century glass in the sanctuary is of St. Anne teaching the Child Virgin to read. C4

· ALL SAINTS ·
PAVEMENT

The 13th century door knocker is said to depict the devil swallowing a woman. The 15th century lectern has one of the few chained books left in England. Medieval glass in the west window shows scenes from The Passion. The Guilds hold their annual services in this church. Its parish hall, St. Crux at Whip-ma-Whop-ma-Gate, contains a magnificently restored monument to Sir Robert Watter, twice Lord Mayor of York, who gave the city the Chain of Office still worn by Lord Mayors today. D/E4

· HOLY TRINITY ·
GOODRAMGATE

One of York's most interesting churches, built between 1250 and 1500. The tower has a rare saddleback, or pitched roof. Notable woodwork includes a Jacobean altar rail, 18th century box pews and a two-decker pulpit. The chapel on the south wall has an old altar stone with crosses for the wounds of Christ. Between the chapel and the main body of the church there is a 'squint,' or hagioscope, a hole in the wall so the priest in the chapel altar can see the High Altar. Ancient glass includes the five-light east window with representations of the Holy Trinity in the centre panels. D2

¶
Holy Trinity, Goodramgate

· HOLY TRINITY ·
MICKLEGATE

A fragment of a great church which was part of the Benedictine Priory from 1089 to 1426. Portions of the Norman church's central tower can be seen near the chancel steps. The medieval Mystery Plays originally began their performance outside the gateway of Holy Trinity Priory, which was demolished in 1856. B5

· ST. CUTHBERT ·
PEASHOLME GREEN

York's second oldest church, dating from 687. Roman stones are incorporated in the building. Not open to the public. E/F2

· ST. DENYS ·
WALMGATE

This church was formerly double its present length. In 1798 the nave was taken down and a new doorway was created: the Norman porch of four recessed Orders carved with quaint figures. The north aisle windows are examples of early 14th century tracery, and the church has some of the oldest glass in York, from the 12th century. E/F4

· ST. HELEN ·
STONEGATE

¶
St Helen, Stonegate

Actually in St. Helen's Square, this is formerly the Guild Church of the medieval glass painters. Built in the 14th century, it has been restored several times and partially rebuilt. 15th century glass in the west window shows St. Helen, St. William, and Edward the Confessor. Victorian glass in the east window shows the Four Evangelists. St. Helen's is now the civic church, where the Lord Mayor and Council annually attend Harvest Thanksgiving in state.

D3

· ST. JOHN THE EVANGELIST ·
MICKLEGATE

First mentioned in 1194, the church's core is the base of a late 12th century tower, notable as the only surviving example in York. The half-timbered belfry, c. 1646, houses four medieval bells and two 17th century ones. Closed in 1934, with the medieval glass being moved to the Minster in 1939, St. John's was restored by York Civic Trust and opened as York Arts Centre in 1968. C4

· ST. MARGARET ·
WALMGATE

Features a fine example of the Yorkshire school of late Norman doorways, with five recessed Orders and ten carved capitals. Closed. F4/5

· ST. MARTIN-CUM-GREGORY ·
MICKLEGATE

Services are no longer held here, but there is still much of interest in this early 13th century church, including ancient glass in the south-west windows. B4/5

· ST. MARTIN-LE-GRAND ·
CONEY STREET

The original church, mainly 15th century, was gutted in an air raid in 1942. The present successful combination of old and new occupies the south aisle of the original, the remainder being a paved garden. It is a shrine of remembrance to the fallen of the two World Wars and all who died in the 1942 raid. The unique modern English organ hanging from the roof was a gift of the German Government and Evangelical Church.

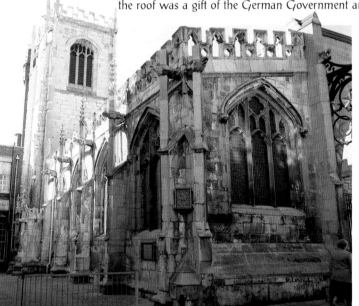

The new east window and the Last Supper sculpture are modern works of art, while the window in the new north wall is one of the finest early 15th century windows in the country. With remarkable foresight, the window had been removed for safety before World War Two.

The great clock which dominates Coney Street is topped by a sailor, known as the Little Admiral.

He is reading an early sextant, and originally rotated with the sun. The face on the side is Father Time. The works are actually inside the church and drive the clock through a shaft. The church's most famous parishioner was Margaret Clitherow, now St. Margaret of York. She was married in this church.C3

· ST. MARY ·
BISHOPHILL JUNIOR

The tower incorporates typical Saxon windows and herringbone brickwork, and the remains of a Saxon cross are preserved inside the church. The aisles were added between the 12th and 14th centuries, the chancel was rebuilt in the 13th century and restored in 1860. B5

· ST. MICHAEL-LE-BELFREY ·
PETERGATE

¶
St Michael-le-Belfrey, Petergate

This fine example of Tudor church architecture was built about 1536, the west end was rebuilt in 1867. There is early 14th century glass in the east window and 16th century glass in the north and south aisles. Guy Fawkes was baptised here on 16th April, 1570. D2

· ST. MICHAEL
SPURRIERGATE

The beautiful interior with late 12th century arcades has a fine 18th century carved panel, a rare chalice brass of the 15th century and interesting medieval glass. D4

· ST. OLAVE ·
MARYGATE

Founded over 900 years ago, but the present church dates mainly from the 18th century, as it was badly damaged during the Civil War. Interesting features include the coat of arms of James I's son Henry, Prince of Wales; and a medieval coffin lid. The tomb of the artist William Etty is in the churchyard. B2

· ST. SAMPSON ·
CHURCH STREET

Largely re-built between 1845 and 1848, the church was in the possession of Pontefract Priory in 1154. Its late 15th century tower was damaged by gunshot in 1644 and not restored until 1910. One panel of medieval glass is incorporated in the west window. The church, closed for services in 1969, was restored and converted into an old people's centre in 1974.

D3

· ST. SAVIOUR'S ·
ST. SAVIOURGATE

Dates back to at least c. 1090 and was, in the main, rebuilt in 1844-5. Features a large 15th century east window, the stained glass for which is now part of All Saints, Pavement. E3

· HOLY REDEEMER ·
BOROUGHBRIDGE ROAD

An interesting marriage of old and new. Built partially from the stones of the former St. Mary Bishophill Senior.

· BURIAL GROUNDS ·

· CHOLERA BURIAL GROUNDS ·

Below the City Wall, opposite the railway station. Tombstones mark graves of the victims of York's last cholera epidemic in the summer of 1832. A4

· CHRIST CHURCH ·
KING'S SQUARE

Old tombstones in the square mark the site of this ancient church, demolished in 1937. D3

· ST. GEORGE'S · CHURCHYARD
GEORGE STREET

Dick Turpin is buried here, under a modern tombstone replacing the original, which had worn away. F5

· ST. HELEN'S BURIAL GROUND ·
DAVYGATE

This was used as a burial ground for St. Helen's after the original churchyard had been destroyed to create St. Helen's Square. D3

· MUSEUMS & CITY ART · GALLERY

· THE BAR CONVENT MUSEUM ·

This has been the site of the Institute of the Blessed Virgin Mary since 1686. During a century of suppression, the nuns survived by keeping a low profile, and though it was illegal, they even ran a Catholic girls' school.

The present building dates from the 1760's. Because Catholic chapels were still illegal, the architect was instructed to completely conceal the beautiful baroque chapel from outside observers. It was designed with nine exits for quick escapes, and there is even a priest's hiding hole under the chapel floor.

In the 19th century, the Convent expanded into Ireland, the nuns began teaching in St. George's Primary school, and they ran a local Boy's Brigade.

During World War Two the east wing buildings were destroyed in an air raid. Today, their modern replacements are part of All Saints Comprehensive School.

The older historic parts of the building now house a Youth Hostel and The Bar Convent Museum, where visitors can take a 'pilgrimage' through three hundred turbulent years of Christianity in York. B5/6

· YORK CASTLE MUSEUM ·

England's most popular museum of everyday life, the Castle Museum remains a "must" for visitors to York.

At its heart the Museum has the amazing collection of objects acquired by Dr. John Kirk, a country doctor in the Yorkshire market town of Pickering. Kirk acquired the collection to represent a way of life that was fast disappearing with the advent of mass production and the move from rural to urban living.

In 1938 the City Council opened the Museum based upon the Kirk Collection. It has since been enlarged and its nostalgic overview extends right up to the 1960's in the new display "Every Home Should Have One." Today, the Museum fills the buildings of the former Female Prison and Debtor's Prison.

Period Displays include a completely decorated 17th century hall, a Georgian Dining Room, Victorian Parlour, a Moorland Cottage and a 1953 Coronation Room.

There's a nostalgic display of household machines and gadgets, from turn of the century lamps, baths and heaters to early phonographs, radios and televisions.

The Founder's Gallery features an interesting comparison of kitchens and their furniture.

In May 1982, during building operations in York, the Coppergate Helmet was discovered. Only the third Anglo-Saxon helmet ever found, this magnificent piece of craftsmanship now on display in the museum was probably made in York more than 1,200 years ago and is the finest example in existence, with brass fittings richly decorated with intricate animals.

'Kirkgate' is an authentically reproduced Victorian street, while Half Moon Court presents a picture of life in the more mechanized Edwardian age. In the prison cells, see where Dick Turpin was held before his execution.

Other cells are now recreated craft workshops of bygone days.

The galleries include a military display of Marston Moor, Costume and Accessory displays and a Children's Gallery.

Outside, Raindale Mill is a working mill from April to October.

E5

¶
Kirkgate,
York Castle Museum

· NATIONAL RAILWAY ·
MUSEUM

One of the biggest railway collections in Britain and one of the best railway museums in the world. The Great Hall features over 25 magnificent locomotives and 20 historic pieces of rolling stock.

Locomotives include a primitive steam locomotive built in 1829; a 'Deltic' diesel-electric; and a full-size steam locomotive with cut-aways to show the interior construction. Amongst the rolling stock is Queen Victoria's Saloon.

¶
Queen Victoria's Carriage

The adjoining galleries offer a wide range of railway-related exhibits, and there is an outdoor display area as well. The museum has a comprehensive education and leisure service, reference library and a photographic service, all available by prior arrangement.

Museum Shop. Refreshment Room. Opening hours: Mon. – Sat. 1000 – 1800. Sun. 1430 – 1800. Closed New Year's Day, Good Friday, Mayday Bank Holiday, Christmas Eve, Christmas Day, Boxing Day.   A3

· WAX MUSEUM ·

On Lower Friargate, the Wax Museum features dozens of tableaux of famous people and incidents from history, complete with special lighting and sound effects.

It is also home to lifesize models of the present Duke and Duchess of York, along with six former Dukes including Frederick Augustus, the renowned Grand Old Duke of York.

¶
The National Railway Museum

The Museum houses some of the country's most important collections of archaeology, natural history, geology and pottery. It has extensive prehistoric, Viking and medieval displays and a superb new Roman Gallery, with many artefacts from York's Roman past. The collections of fossils, rocks and minerals are of national significance, the Museum's displays of mammals and birds give a complete picture of Yorkshire wildlife and there is also a very large entomological collection.

The Museum Botanical Gardens were laid out in the grounds of the ruined St. Mary's Abbey in the early 19th century. In addition to many interesting varieties of trees and plants, the grounds contain parts of the City Walls, the ruins of St. Leonard's Hospital and the Multangular Tower. The famous Mystery Plays are also performed here against the dramatic backdrop of the Abbey ruins. B2

Recreation of Roman kitchen
¶

· YORKSHIRE MUSEUM · OF FARMING

The museum brings alive the history of farming and countryside life through the ages. See regular demonstrations of spinning, weaving, corn dolly making, butter making and stonewalling. Learn how the seasons affect life on the land; in the Four Seasons Building. Pet the pigs, calves and sheep in the Livestock Building and visit the reconstructed weaver's cottage, shepherd's hut and turn of the century ironmonger's shop.

Among the many exhibits are a range of early and modern tractors, giant threshing machines and hundreds of tools and utensils. Set in eight acres of country park at Murton, three miles from York. Won the award for Best Museum of Social and Industrial History in the 1985 Museum of the Year Awards.

Open to the public between March and the end of October, with special events at Bank Holiday weekends.

· YORK CITY ART GALLERY ·

The City Art Gallery dominates Exhibition Square just outside Bootham Bar and enjoys an international reputation for the quality and presentation of its extensive collection. This dates from 1350 to the present

day and covers most of the countries of western Europe. The gallery is particularly famous for the Lycett Green collection of Old Masters. There is also an important collection of British paintings from the 16th to the 20th centuries, including a substantial group of works by the York-born artist William Etty.

One collection, largely devoted to the topography of York, includes a great many water-colours, drawings and prints, and many of the famous British water-colour artists are represented. An important collection of modern stoneware is also featured in the gallery.

The Gallery provides a lively programme of temporary exhibitions, lectures, recitals and other events. These are announced in the Gallery bulletin and are also advertised locally. Children are welcome in the gallery, and special "picture spotting" sheets are available to help them enjoy their visits. Special events including painting sessions and craft workshops are held during the holidays. Free admission. C2

· JORVIK VIKING ·
CENTRE

One of York's most popular attractions. The Jorvik Viking Centre in Coppergate is an exact reconstruction of life in Viking York, based on the results of five years of painstaking archaeological excavation.

A special 'time car' will take you on a journey back through a thousand years to the days when Viking villagers lived in tiny huts on this site.

The sights, sounds and smells of a bustling Viking community are recreated. Along the way, you'll see the carefully preserved excavation, a display from many of the artefacts which were found.

The Jorvik Viking Centre, a unique journey into York's Viking past. D4

· YORK STORY ·
YORK'S HERITAGE
CENTRE

This intriguing and original centre is run by York City Council and is an absolute must for the visitor. The centre is both an enjoyable and educational way to explore 1,000 years of York's history and architecture. A delightful mixture of scale models, intricate drawings, detailed paintings and audio-visual presentations guide you through York's varied history and its many building styles.

The numerous displays include "Treasures of the City," with an outstanding selection of Mansion House silver.

And one towering exhibit gives you a real insight into the precarious nature of medieval cathedral construction.

Located in the former St. Mary's Church on Castlegate, near the Jorvik Viking Centre.

Illustrated guide book available. D4

A Gilt Inn Sign at the York Story
¶

· THE RIVERS ·

York was a major port and trading centre for centuries. The Ouse was tidal here until 1757, and York was head of navigation for sea-going vessels. The Foss was dammed by William the Conqueror to protect his castles, provide power for corn mills, and to create a fishpond for the King. Now, the Ouse provides the city with over ten million gallons of water a day. Barges, pleasure launches and rowing boats regularly use the river, and there are regattas every summer.

Along the river-banks there are pleasant walks and delightful picnic spots.

From the Lendal Bridge, there is a path along the east bank of the Ouse, past the Museum Gardens and the City Wall to the suburb of Clifton, where a bus runs back into the city centre.

On the other side of the bridge, start at the steps below the North Street Postern Tower and follow North Street to the riverside garden opposite the Guildhall. This is where the Roman bridge crossed the river. The walk continues along the riverbank in front of the Viking Hotel to Ouse Bridge.

Across the Ouse Bridge, steps lead down onto King's Staith and the South Esplanade to St. George's Gardens and the Castle area. Through St. George's Gardens there is a pleasant walk under Skeldergate Bridge to St. George's Field. Continue along the riverside path to the Blue Bridge, where the Foss joins the Ouse. Cross the tiny bridge, and walk along the Ouse again to Fulford Ings. You can catch a bus back into York from the Fulford road nearby.

From Lendal Bridge and South Esplanade there are one hour return river cruises to Bishopthorpe. Rowing boats can be hired at Lendal Bridge.

· UNIVERSITY OF YORK ·

Most of the University is located on a lovely 190-acre campus at Heslington, just outside the city boundary. When it opened in 1963 there were 216 undergraduates and 12 graduate students, today the student population numbers around 4,000.

The administrative offices are housed in Heslington Hall, an Elizabethan mansion rebuilt in the 19th century. Other notable and more recent buildings on the campus include the Central Hall, the Sir Jack Lyons Concert Hall, the J.B. Morrell Library, the Language Centre and the Chemistry, Biology and Physics/Electronics laboratories. The Borthwick Institute of Historical Research in St. Anthony's Hall, Aldwark and the Institute of Advanced Architectural Studies in King's Manor are also part of the University.

The University has recently established a number of commercial enterprises, offers services to industry and government and has become a major centre for conferences. Many of its activities, including concerts and theatre, societies and lecture series, and athletic facilities, are open to the public.

Visitors are welcome to walk around the beautifully landscaped campus with its delightful artificial lake. Regular bus routes go to the University, and visitors arriving by car are welcome to use the free University car parks.

· EVENTS ·
& ENTERTAINMENTS

· THE YORK FESTIVAL ·
& MYSTERY PLAYS

The major cultural event in York is the Quadrennial Festival, next taking place in 1988. It has acquired an enviable reputation as one of the country's leading festivals and offers a densely-packed programme of arts and entertainment lasting three weeks.

The centrepiece of the Festival is the York cycle of Mystery Plays. These were originally written and performed by the city's ancient craft guilds, beginning in 1340. Each guild had its own play, performed from a wagon, and the cycle spanned the whole Bible Story from Creation to the Last Judgement.

¶
'Mystery Plays, 1951' –
Raymond Teague Cowen

The plays were presented every year on Corpus Christi in June. The wagons were pulled through the city streets, each stopping at a dozen points en route to perform.

Today, the Mystery Plays are staged at a specially created arena among the ruins of St. Mary's Abbey. The original texts have been retained and the performers are still almost entirely the people of York themselves. The Mystery Plays are a compelling and moving experience and now attract thousands of people from around the world.

· THE YORK EARLY MUSIC ·
FESTIVAL

Held annually, except during the Quadrennial Festival, the York Festival of Early Music has earned a distinguished reputation in its few short years. The Festival's lively and unusual programme of concerts, workshops and other events is designed to appeal to both specialist and general audiences alike.

· THE THEATRE ROYAL ·
ST LEONARD'S PLACE

There has been a theatre here for over two centuries. Today, the resident professional company performs all year round, everything from classic drama to modern comedy. The programme also includes opera, musicals and concerts. Performances seven nights a week. Restaurant and Bar. C2

THE · ARTS · CENTRE

In St. John The Evangelist Church, Micklegate.

Offers a varied programme including drama, films, live music, poetry and dance, all in the intimate setting of the former St. John's Church. Restaurant and Bar. C4

· UNIVERSITY OF YORK ·

The University presents an annual series of orchestral concerts and recitals. The York Film Theatre is also based there and has a regular programme of quality films. The University is located just outside the city boundary and is easily reached by car or bus. For programme details, consult the local press.

· CITY OF YORK · LEISURE SERVICES

A Department of York City Council which promotes a wide range of entertainment and activities throughout the year.

Included are concerts and light entertainment; spectacular city centre sports events, such as grand prix athletics and professional cycling; and major outdoor events like the York Festival of Kites.

Further information from the Department at the Red House, Duncombe Place, York YO1 2EF.

· YORK CITY ART GALLERY ·

Also part of City of York Leisure Services, providing lunchtime entertainment on alternate Tuesdays throughout the year. These hour-long events are a welcome break for city workers and visitors alike.

· TOURIST INFORMATION · CENTRE & LIBRARY

ST LEONARD'S PLACE & MUSEUM STREET

To find out more about what's on in York visit the Tourist Information Centre or the Library. They have a vast selection of brochures on local events and activities, and helpful people to answer your questions.

'Fine Art Exhibition Building, York' – J Stead after Brown
¶

· SPORT FOR THE · VISITOR

Whether you wish to be an active participant or just a spectator, York offers an excellent variety of sporting opportunities.

· ANGLING ·

York is situated on the River Ouse and a good variety of coarse fishing is available in waters around York.

· BOWLS ·

There are numerous bowling greens located in parks and gardens around the city. For more information, contact the Leisure Services Department.*

· CRICKET ·

Yorkshire's traditional ruling passion. The city's premier club, York Cricket Club, play club cricket at Clifton Park, Shipton Road.

· FOOTBALL ·

York City Football Club play in the English Football League at their Bootham Crescent ground. The soccer season is from late August to early May.

· GLIDING ·

Ouse Gliding Club fly at weekends and on Bank Holidays throughout the year. The club is located at Rufforth Airfield, five miles from York on the Wetherby Road (B.1224).

· GOLF ·

Yorkshire is one of England's great golfing counties, and there are four courses in and around York. Fulford, probably the best known, is the home of occasional major events. York Golf Club at Strensall is well worth a visit. There are also smaller courses at Heworth and Pike Hills.

· HORSERACING ·

York Racecourse, located on the Knavesmire, is the premier racecourse in the north. There are five race meetings a year between May and October. The most famous is in August during "Ebor Week" and is one of the major classics on the racing calendar.

· RAMBLING ·

The Ramblers' Association organize a 10-12 mile weekend ramble of least once a month, evening mid-week walks during the summer and Wednesday walks at fortnightly intervals. For further details, contact the Tourist Information Centre.

· ROWING ·

York City Rowing Club provide all year round Rowing and Sculling facilities from their Boat House on the West Esplanade. The Club also organize regattas on the Ouse each May and June.

· RUGBY LEAGUE ·

York Rugby League Football Club play professional Rugby League at their Clarence Street ground between September and April.

· RUGBY UNION ·

York Rugby Union Football Club play at Clifton Park, Shipton Road, between April and September.

· SAILING ·

There are sailing clubs on the Ouse at Naburn and Acaster Malbis, both 4 miles outside York. Spectators are welcome, especially during races.

· SWIMMING ·

The city's three swimming pools include the Barbican Swimming Pool, conveniently located close to the city centre. The Barbican has three pools, a fitness unit and a sauna/sunbed suite.

¶
Festival of Kites

· SQUASH ·

There are facilities at Oaklands Sports Centre, which has no membership restrictions and welcomes visitors.

· TENNIS ·

There are numerous tennis courts located around the city. Contact the Leisure Services Department.*

* The City Council, through its Leisure Services Department, provides a wide range of amenities for both local residents and visitors to the city. Contact the Leisure Services Department, The Red House, Duncombe Place, York, YO1 2EF.

· DINING & DRINKING ·

York is brimming with fine restaurants, bistros, tea rooms and pubs.

Some of the ancient inns and taverns date back to the early 17th century and many are reputed to be haunted, such as the Yorkshire Hussar on North Street.

Sample traditional, regional and national cuisine. York offers a varied menu to suit pocket and palate alike.

¶
Ye Olde Starre

· WHERE TO STAY ·

The City of York offers accommodation as varied as its visitors from all over the world.

From friendly Guesthouses to Hotels of international repute, the warmth of welcome and standards are as renowned as the beauty and history of the City itself.

Of invaluable help to the visitor seeking accommodation is the "Where to Stay Guide" available from the Tourist Information Centre, De Grey Rooms, Exhibition Square.

Royal York Hotel
¶

· SHOPPING ·

From unique local shops with character to the major multiples, one of York's great attractions is the variety and quality of its shops. The visitor can find much to take home that is rare, beautiful and often distinctive.

Antiques, fine porcelain and crystal, militaria, ancient pottery or crafts, to fine foodstores and quality clothing, York has them all.

On virtually every street corner and lining its winding streets, you'll discover York is truly a shoppers' paradise.

¶
Shambles at Night

· BOOKS ABOUT YORK ·

· GENERAL GUIDES ·

· BARTHOLOMEW CITY GUIDES - YORK ·
J. Hutchinson & D.W. Palliser – 1980 J. Bartholomew & Son 332 pages.

· THE NOBLE CITY OF YORK ·
Herald Printers – 1972 – Westminster Press 1044 pages.

· PORTRAIT OF YORK ·
Ronald Willis – 1972 – Robert Hale 209 pages.

· A WALK AROUND · THE SNICKLEWAYS OF YORK
Mark Jones – 1986 – Mark & Anne Jones 92 pages.

· YORK ·
Angela Fiddes – 1985 – Pevensey Press 96 pages.

· YORK ·
Peter Wenham – 1971 – Longman 176 pages.

· CITY OF YORK ·
STREET MAP

Throughout the Guide wherever possible, attractions of particular interest have been given a reference to aid location on the map opposite e.g. The Minster D2.

 CAR PARKS

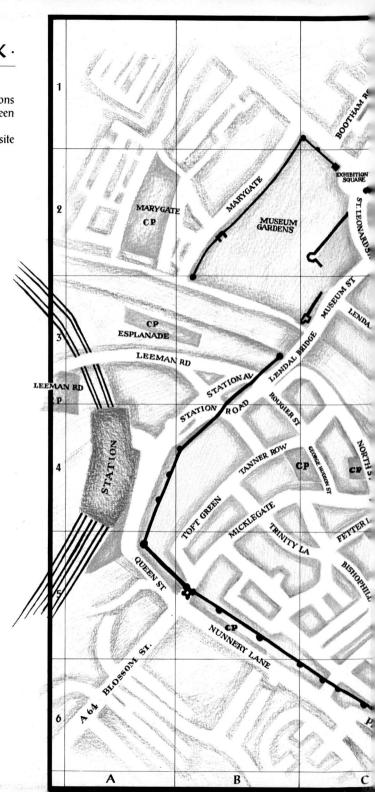

· ACKNOWLEDGMENTS ·

¶ York City Council would like to thank the many people whose assistance made the production of The Official Guide possible, in particular The Chapter Clerk's Office, York Minster; York Archaeological Trust. ¶ The illustrations and photographs used throughout The Guide are copyright and may not be reproduced in any form without the prior permission of the following: Contents Page, Woodmansterne Picture Library, Watford. Page 8, York Archaeological Trust. Page 9, Cultural Resource Management. Page 11, (Right) York Archaeological Trust. Page 12, City of York, Department of Leisure Services. Page 13, City Art Gallery, City of York Leisure Services. Pages 14 & 15, City Art Gallery, City of York Leisure Services. Page 16, (Bottom) Borodin Communications, York. Page 17, (Top) British Telecom (Bottom) John Rylands University Library, Manchester. Page 18, City Art Gallery, City of York Leisure Services. Page 20, (Bottom) Woodmansterne Picture Library, Watford. Pages 22 & 23 City Art Gallery, City of York Leisure Services. Page 25, (Top) City Art Gallery, City of York Leisure Services (Bottom) Woodmansterne Picture Library, Watford. Page 26, City Art Gallery, City of York Leisure Services. Page 27, City Art Gallery, City of York Leisure Services. Pages 28 & 29, Woodmansterne Picture Library, Watford. Page 30, City Art Gallery, City of York Leisure Services. Pages 31, 32 & 33, Woodmansterne Picture Library, Watford. Page 37, Woodmansterne, Picture Library, Watford. Page 38 (Top) City Art Gallery, City of York Leisure Services.. Page 39, (Top) Woodmansterne Picture Library, Watford (Bottom) City Art Gallery, City of York Leisure Services. Pages 40 & 41, City Art Gallery, City of York Leisure Services. Page 42, (Bottom) Woodmansterne Picture Library, Watford. Page 47, (Top) Woodmansterne Picture Library, Watford. Page 48, (Top) Judges Postcards Limited, Sussex (Bottom) Woodmansterne Picture Library, Watford. Page 49, City Art Gallery, City of York Leisure Services. Pages 50, (Top) J Salmon Ltd, Kent (Bottom) Woodmansterne, Picture Library, Watford. Page 51, (Bottom) City Art Gallery, City of York Leisure Services. Page 56, York Archaeological Trust. Page 57, Castle Museum, City of York Leisure Services. Page 58, (Top) National Railway Museum, York (Bottom) Woodmansterne Picture Library, Watford. Page 59, Yorkshire Museum. Pages 60 & 61, City Art Gallery, City of York Leisure Services. Page 62, Jorvik Viking Centre. Page 64, (Top) City Art Gallery, City of York Leisure Services. Page 65, Borodin Communications. Page 66, City Art Gallery, City of York Leisure Services. Page 68, City Art Gallery, City of York Leisure Services. Page 69, City of York Leisure Services. Page 72, (Bottom Right) Format Publications, York. All others, City of York. ¶ Front Cover Illustration, Jack Henshaw. ¶ Additional Illustrations, Alan Young and Tony Jones. ¶ Additional Photography, Chris Rose. ¶ Co-ordinated, designed and produced by Luckett & Co (0532) 448651.